D1556871

Songs of Cifar and the Sweet Sea

A Center for Inter-American Relations Book

Pablo Antonio Cuadra

Songs of Cifar and the Sweet Sea

*Selections from "Songs of Cifar,
1967–1977"*

Translated and Edited by
Grace Schulman and Ann McCarthy de Zavala

Published by
Columbia University Press

in association with the
Center for Inter-American Relations

New York / 1979

Assistance in the publication of this volume was given by the
Center for Inter-American Relations. The Center acknowledges
the support of the New York State Council on the Arts
in the preparation of the translation.

Printed in the United States of America

Library of Congress Cataloging in Publication Data

Cuadra, Pablo Antonio, 1912–
    Songs of Cifar and the sweet sea.

    English and Spanish.
    "A Center for Inter-American Relations book."
    I. Title.
PQ7519.C8A27   861   79-4115
ISBN 0-231-04772-X
ISBN 0-231-04773-8 pbk.

iv

A CARLOS, mi hermano
—que vivió como pocos la vida
y la aventura de la gente de
nuestro Mar Dulce—.
Y en memoria de Cifar Guevara
alias El Cachero; de Juan de Dios
Mora; de Felipe Potoy y de Sinforosa
Salablanca, su mujer; de mi compadre
Leonidas Cruz, de Pascasio, de Eladio,
de Cristóbal, todos finados, que en
paz descansen, compañeros de mi ju-
ventud navegante.

To Carlos, my brother, who lived as few have done
the adventurous life of the people of our Sweet
Sea. And in memory of Cifar Guevara, alias The
Cockroach; of Juan de Dios Mora; of Felipe Potoy
and of Sinforosa Salablanca, his wife; of Leonidas
Cruz, father of my godchild; of Pascasio; of Eladio;
of Cristóbal; all deceased; that they may rest in
peace, companions of my navigating youth.

V

Acknowledgments

Thirty-four of the poems from "Songs of Cifar and the Sweet Sea" were published originally in *The Hudson Review,* 30, no. 4 (Winter 1977). They are, the prologue, "Sailor's Barcarole," "The Birth of Cifar," "Horses in the Lake," "The Sickness," "The Departure," "Cries," "The Master of Tarca (I, III, IV, V and VII)," "The Girls," "Manuscript in a Bottle," "The Call," "Eufemia," "Angelina on the Cliffs," "Abduction," "Writing on a Tree," "The Child," "The Wedding of Cifar," "That's My Woman," "The Letter," "Message to Christopher," "The Rebel," "Tomasito the Cook," "Ducks," "The Island of the Gavilanes," "Cifar's Nostalgia," "Mirna," "Misfortune," "The Procession," "Written by Cifar about his Daughter, Ubaldina" and "Fisherman."

Seven of the poems appeared originally in *Translation,* 5 (Spring 1978). They are, "The Islands," "The Evening Star," "Consolation for the Mother of the Fisherman," "The Empty Island," "In Memoriam," "The Cemetery of Birds" and "Farewell."

Some of the translations have been revised since their first appearance. The Spanish and the English versions were read at the Center for Inter-American Relations by Pablo Antonio Cuadra and Grace Schulman on April 15, 1977.

The translators are grateful for the help and encouragement of Frederick Morgan and Paula Deitz, of *The Hudson Review;* Ronald Christ, Gregory Kolovakos and Rosario Santos, of the Center for Inter-American Relations; Jessica Hirchbein; Jerome Schulman; and Xavier Zavala. They wish to thank Willard Trask for his wise counsel, and for his exemplary achievement.

Contents

xi

Introduction

Pablo Antonio Cuadra: Poet
of the Nicaraguan Vanguard

Pablo Antonio Cuadra, one of Nicaragua's leading poets, was born in Managua, Nicaragua, in 1912, the son of Doña Mercedes Cardenal and Dr. Carlos Cuadra Pasos. Cuadra spent much of his life in Granada, where the family moved when he was four years old.

In his childhood, the poet spent vacations on ranches and country estates, growing familiar with the Nicaraguan landscape. Later, he studied law but abandoned that profession to write about the land. Working as a farmer and cattle-raiser on family farms near Lake Nicaragua, he was drawn to the lives and manners of the Lake people. He navigated through those waters for twenty years, meeting peasants, fishermen, sailors, woodcutters, and timber merchants.

Cuadra suffered through his country's political struggles from an early age. Before he was twenty, he felt keenly the humiliating presence of the United States Marines, who were stationed in Nicaragua for seventeen years. The young writer was inspired by Augusto César Sandino, the guerrilla fighter who continued his warfare in the northern mountains until the Marines were withdrawn in 1933. Driven by nationalist feeling and a deep desire for Nicaraguan independence, Cuadra backed General Anastasio Somoza, father of the present General Somoza, in the hope of initiating a new Nicaragua freed of its false sense of equality and safe from foreign intervention. In 1946, however, disillusioned by the dictatorship of the elder Somoza, Cuadra left Nicaragua for Mexico and Spain, where he described himself as a "voluntary exile." He taught poetry and read his work at various universities in the United States and in South America, then returned home in 1950.

Cuadra's concern with national affairs generated his career in journalism. Cuadra is editor of *La Prensa* of Managua, one of the most outspoken newspapers of Central America. His column on cultural matters, "Escrito a Máquina" ("typewritten," as opposed to his poetry, which is handwritten), indicates the division within himself between journalism's immediate impact and art's permanence. He is also editor of *La Prensa Literaria,* the Sunday section of *La Prensa* devoted to the arts, which presents established writers and gifted new ones. Of the many literary journals he has founded and edited, *El Pez y la Serpiente,* started in 1960, remains alive and under his direction. It is an outstanding periodical.

The poetry of Pablo Antonio Cuadra incarnates his dream of an autonomous Nicaragua. Wisely, he is never didactic; instead, he sings his country's music and folklore, celebrating its villages and farms. His first book, *Poemas nicaragüenses (Nicaraguan Poems)* appeared in 1934 when he was twenty-two years old. It was the initial book of poetry from the *Vanguardia,* or Nicaraguan literary vanguard, a movement dedicated to renewing the country's writing. Inaugurated in 1927 by another young poet, José Coronel Urtecho, the Vanguardia included Joaquin Pasos as well, and those writers, with Cuadra, became masters in a Nicaraguan literary renaissance. Because the styles of those artists varied considerably, the movement was never a school. It was, however, a force in creating a literature free from European influence, which was an artistic fulfillment of the political wish to liberate Nicaragua from foreign intervention.

Cuadra's *Nicaraguan Poems* heralded that rebirth of his country's poetry, for it embodied common speech, Nicaraguan customs, and ordinary objects. His art was not in the Modernist movement inaugurated by the Nicaraguan poet Rubén Darío, whose metaphors referred commonplace things to a realm of ethereal splendor, but in the powerful indigenous tradition of the vanguard group. The books of his exile—*La Tierra prometida* (*The Promised Land*, composed in 1952), and *Libro de horas* (*The Book of Hours*, 1956), never lost their national identification. And *El Jaguar y la luna* (*The Jaguar & the Moon*, 1959), a book that is built on his country's powerful Indian legends, won the Rubén Darío prize for Central American verse in 1959, and was translated into English by Thomas Merton.[1] Although his work has been published in Portuguese (in Brazil), and in Italian, *The Jaguar & The Moon* is the only book-length English version of his poetry.

Like Ernesto Cardenal, the priest who founded a community to serve the poor on the Island of Solentiname, Pablo Antonio Cuadra feels an impassioned unity with the peasants and laborers of Nicaragua; in his poetry, he identifies with the *campesinos* he has lived and worked among. Cardenal wrote: "Pablo Antonio in his poetry has given universal transcendence to the packsaddle, the flat pan, the grindstone. . . ."[2] And like Cardenal, Cuadra writes out of a profound spiritual conviction. After his active political period, and his disillusionment with the elder Somoza, Cua-

1. *La Tierra prometida* (Managua: El Hilo Azul, 1952); *Libro de Horas: Antología de la poesía católica del siglo XX* (Madrid: A. Vasallo, 1964); *El Jaguar y la luna* (Buenos Aires: Ediciones Carlos Lohlé, 1971). The last book was translated into English as *The Jaguar & the Moon* (Greensboro, N.C.: The Unicorn Press, 1971), reprinted from *Emblems of a Season of Fury* (New York: New Directions, 1963).
2. "Pablo Antonio Cuadra visto por Ernesto Cardenal," in *Repertorio latino-americano*, Buenos Aires (July 1975), p. 4.

dra went through a severe spiritual crisis that was reflected in *Canto temporal* (*Temporal Song,* 1943), a long poem that appeared as a bound volume reprinted from the periodical, *Cuaderno del Taller San Lucas.*[3] Of that inner conflict, Cuadra wrote: "I used to have faith in the Faith—but this decisive encounter with Christ revealed to me faith in love."[4] The Nicaraguan poet found Christ in the people, believing that their labors would bring about a new dawn of peace. And so ends "The Islands," from *Songs of Cifar,* a poem dedicated to his friend, Ernesto Cardenal:

> Se oyen lejanos
> los gallos.
>> El viento
> sopla en la brasa del lucero.
> Parece
> que ya amanece.

> The cocks
> are heard in the distance.
>> The wind
> blows on the hot coal of the morning star.
> Already it seems to be dawn.

"Songs of Cifar and the Sweet Sea" is a selection from *Songs of Cifar,* which appeared in two editions, in 1969 and in 1971, and then in a complete edition that year. The cycle of poems recounts the odyssey of a mariner, Cifar, who, with a "thirst for horizons," travels around the waters and islands of Lake Nicaragua. That body of water, variously called "The Lake" and "The Great Lake," is fresh water ("sweet sea")

3. Num. 3, Granada, 1943.
4. Quoted in *Tierra que habla: Antología de cantos nicaragüenses* (San Jose, Costa Rica: Editorial Universitaria Centroamericana, 1974), p. 176.

that is, wondrously, filled with dangerous sharks and shad. One of two freshwater lakes in Nicaragua, it is 92 miles long and 34 miles wide. Its Indian name is Cocibolca, meaning "the place or nest of the Great Serpent."

In *Songs of Cifar,* Cuadra writes of the people he worked among: the sailors who dry their nets in the sun, the fishermen who smell the smoke of breakfast, the merchants, the owners of sailboats, the sailors who row in gentle winds and in storms, insulting the rain and the waves. He writes of Eladio, the river carpenter; Mirna, the prostitute; Pascasio, the one-armed sailor; Mora, the hog-raiser; Lalita, the brothel-keeper. He writes of herons, white sails, sardines hurled on the beach, of the cormorants, the cliffs, and, always, of the dead, the hungry, the poor, the shipwrecked in body and in spirit.

Songs of Cifar is at once an epic and a genesis. The poet creates the sense that he is seeing everything in his world for the first time: The Lake is at once real and mythical, so great is his capacity for wonder. And the songs are passionate and lyrical: he uses a vocabulary that is plain and also elevated to an epic tone.

Although Cuadra portrays real people of the present, disclosing actual names of families and places, he uses Greek mythology as the background of the narrative. And in "the Great Lake" that is also the Aegean, modern characters are reminiscent of such figures as the sirens, Circe, Paris, and Helen.

In his poetry, Cuadra makes original use of a greater American tradition that has informed the work of Octavio Paz and César Vallejo, as well as Walt Whitman and Ezra Pound. Cuadra envisions the vast empty areas of space that are central to many poets born in the Americas. Further, he creates an explorer who identifies with the horizon he pursues. Cifar, like Pound's *periplum,* is a voyager who searches for new vistas, new lands. He resembles Whitman's seeing speaker of *Leaves of Grass* who identifies with every leaf, star, and atom. And he is like the seeing speaker of "Prologue," among many poems by Octavio Paz, who sees nature as an organic part of the soul.

In that larger American tradition, Cuadra writes of commonplace objects and things. He depicts natural phenomena with startling accuracy and in presentative detail. In "Ducks," those birds are at once real and transcendent, flying

> como una larga
> flecha
> arrojada al horizonte
> recuperan
> en la altura
> el orden
> la libertad
> y el canto.

> like a long
> arrow
> hurled at the horizon
> recovering
> at that altitude
> order
> freedom
> and song.

In that greater American tradition, Cuadra's poetry incarnates a belief in a remote hidden beauty dominating the concern with things of this world, however precisely those real phenomena are given. And, in the manner that Ezra

xviii

Pound heralded early in the century, he creates an immediate present with undercurrents of his country's past, of myth, and of the classics. In composing a poetry of Nicaraguan Nicaragua, Cuadra has created a poetry of the Americas and, beyond that, of the world.

Grace Schulman

Baruch College,
C.U.N.Y.

Songs of Cifar and the Sweet Sea

"No es extraño en las aguas
de la noche un canto.
   Baja el marinero velas,
   se detiene el remero.
Es Cifar solitario, a la deriva
dejándose llevar de la música y del viento."

(barcarola marinera)

"It is not strange to hear
a song on the night waters.
   The sailor lowers the sails,
   the oarsman pauses.
It is Cifar, alone, adrift,
yielding
to music and wind."

(Sailor's Barcarole)

3

El nacimiento de Cifar

Hay una isla en el playón
pequeña
como la mano de un dios indígena.
Ofrece frutas rojas
a los pájaros
y al náufrago
la dulce sombra de un árbol.
Allí nació Cifar, el navegante
cuando a su madre
se le llegó su fecha, solitaria
remando a Zapatera.
Metió el bote en el remanso
mientras giraban en las aguas
tiburones y sábalos
atraídos por la sangre.

The Birth of Cifar

There is an island in the shallows
slender
as the hand of an Indian god.
It offers red fruit
to the birds
and, to the shipwrecked,
the sweet shade of trees.
There Cifar, the sailor,
was born.
His mother's time came
as she rowed alone to Zapatera.
She steered the boat to a pool
while sharks and shad
circled,
drawn by the blood.

Caballos en el Lago

Los caballos bajan al amanecer.

Entran al lago de oro y avanzan
—ola contra ola
el enarcado cuello y crines—
a la cegadora claridad.
Muchachos desnudos
bañan sus ancas
    y ellos yerguen
    ebrios de luz
su estampa antigua.
Escuchan
—la oreja atenta—
el sutil clarín de la mañana
y miran
el vasto campo de batalla.
Entonces sueñan
    —bulle
    la remota osadía—
se remontan
a los días heroicos
cuando el hierro
devolvía al sol sus lanzas
potros blancos
escuadrones de plata
y el grito
lejanísimo de los pájaros
y el viento.

Horses in the Lake

The horses go down at dawn.

They enter the golden lake and move on—
wave against wave
of arched necks and manes—
into the dazzling light.
Naked boys
bathe their haunches
    and they raise
    their antique figures,
drunk with light.
They listen,
ears attentive,
to the delicate bugle of morning,
and see
the vast battlefield.
Then they dream—
    a remote boldness
    breaks through—
soaring back
to the heroic days
when swords
returned the sun's thrusts,
white stallions
squadrons of silver
and distant cries
of birds
and wind.

Pero vuelven

    (Látigo
    es el tiempo)

Al golpe
enfilan hacia tierra
—bajan la frente—
y uncido
    al carro
      el sueño
queda
    atrás
      dormido
        el viento.

But they return

      (Time
      is the whip)

With the lash
they file toward land,
heads bowed,
and yoked
      to the wagon
       the dream
remains
      behind;
       the wind's
        asleep.

Canturreo en el muelle

Las señoritas
admiran
el atardecer.
Enternecidas
hablan de las nubes
—feas nubes
que amenazan la noche—
Las señoritas
        cantan
con voz fina
y yo, tirando
el anzuelo en el agua
crecida.
        Las señoritas
        enamoradas
        esperan cita
        en la tarde
Los peces no pican
y cae el día
con hambre.

Humming on the Pier

     The young ladies
admire
the late afternoon.
Moved,
they speak of the clouds
that threaten the night . . .
The young ladies
       sing
with delicate voices
and I, casting
my bait in the swollen
water . . .
     The young ladies
     in love
     wait for dates
     in the afternoon.
The fish do not bite
and the day ends
in hunger.

El mal

¿Qué me pide partir?
Los dedos en el arpa
y ya me empieza
el mal de lontananza.

Una
    vela
      lejos
        basta

The Sickness

What urges me to leave?
Fingers in the harp,
and at once there begins
the thirst for horizons.

One
    sail
      afar
        is enough

Dijo la madre a Cifar:
    —¡Deja las aguas!
Sonó Cifar el caracol
y riéndose exclamó:
    —El Lago es aventura.
    —Prefieres, dijo ella
lo temerario a lo seguro.
    —Prefiero
lo extraño a lo conocido.
lzó Cifar los foques
y el solo ruido loco de palomas
    de la vela
lo llenó de alegría.
    —Madre: habla en tu lengua
      el techo estable, la casa,
      la mujer. (Dicen
      que las islas son tumbas de mujeres).
    El hombre es nave.
        —¡Es riesgo!, gritó ella.
Cifar sonrió; puso el arpa en la proa
y doblando el torso tiró de la cadena
    y levó el ancla.
        Otra vez un niño
salía del vientre de su madre
        al mundo . . .

The Departure

Said Cifar's mother:
    —Leave the waters!
Cifar sounded a conch
and, laughing, exclaimed:
    —The Lake is adventure.
    —You prefer, she said,
the risk to safety.
    —I prefer
the strange to the known.
Cifar hoisted a jib
and just the sail's
crazy dovelike sound
filled him with joy.
        —Mother: your language speaks
        of the solid roof, home,
        woman. (They say
        the islands are women's tombs.)
        Men are ships.
    —Men are risks! she cried.
Cifar smiled; putting the harp in the prow
and twisting his body he pulled at the chain
        and raised anchor.
        Once more a child
left his mother's womb
        for the world . . .

En la noche
mientras navegábamos

estuvimos escuchando cantos
muy lejos de tierra.

Una estrella hería
las aguas oscuras
donde naufragaron
las tres muchachas de Tarca
tocadoras de guitarra.

Voices

In the night
while we sailed

we listened to songs
very far from land.

A star wounded
the dark waters
where they had sunk:
the three girls from Tarca,
guitar players.

El maestro de Tarca (I)

Sentado en la piedra del Águila
el maestro de Tarca nos decía:

Es conveniente
es recto
que el marinero
tenga cogidas
las cosas por su nombre.
En el peligro
son las cosas sin nombre
las que dañan.

The Master of Tarca (I)

Seated on the stone of the Eagle
the Master of Tarca would tell us:

It is fitting
and right
that the sailor
grasp
things by their names.
In time of danger ·
things without names
are those that harm.

Las muchachas

Las muchachas del archipiélago
Vuelven de misa remando.
Como flores flotantes
como guirnaldas
de colores alegres.
Diles adiós
desde tu isla
y levantarás un vuelo
de voces frescas
como pájaros.

The Girls

The girls of the archipelago
return from mass
rowing
like floating flowers
like garlands
in bright colors.
Greet them
from your island
and you will raise a flight
of fresh cries
like birds.

Manuscrito en una botella

Yo había mirado los cocoteros y los tamarindos
y los mangos
las velas blancas secándose al sol
el humo del desayuno sobre el cielo
del amanecer
y los peces saltando en la atarraya
y una muchacha vestida de rojo
que bajaba a la playa y subía con el cántaro
y pasaba detrás de la arboleda
y aparecía y desaparecía
y durante mucho tiempo
yo no podía navegar sin esa imagen
de la muchacha vestida de rojo
y los cocoteros y los tamarindos y los mangos
me parecía que sólo existían
porque ella existía
y las velas blancas sólo eran blancas
cuando ella se reclinaba
con su vestido rojo y el humo era celeste
y felices los peces y los reflejos de los peces
y durante mucho tiempo quise escribir un poema
sobre esa muchacha vestida de rojo
y no encontraba el modo de describir
aquella extraña cosa que me fascinaba
y cuando se lo contaba a mis amigos se reían
pero cuando navegaba y volvía
siempre pasaba por la isla de la muchacha de vestido rojo
hasta que un día entré en la bahía de su isla
y eché el ancla y salté a tierra

Manuscript in a Bottle

I had seen coconut trees and tamarinds
and mangos
the white sails drying in the sun
the smoke of breakfast across the sky
at dawn
and fish jumping in the net
and a girl in red
who would go down to the shore and come up with a jug
and pass behind a grove
and appear and disappear
and for a long time
I could not sail without that image
of the girl in red
and the coconut trees and tamarinds and mangos
that seemed to live only
because she lived
and the white sails were white only
when she lay down
in her red dress and the smoke was blue
and the fish and the reflection of the fish
were happy
and for a long time I wanted to write a poem
about that girl in red
and couldn't find the way to describe
the strange thing that fascinated me
and when I told my friends they laughed
but when I sailed away and returned
I always passed the island of the girl in red
until one day I entered the bay of her island
and cast anchor and leaped to land

y ahora escribo estas liíneas y las lanzo a las olas en una
    botella
porque ésta es mi historia
porque estoy mirando los cocoteros y los tamarindos
y los mangos
las velas blancas secándose al sol
y el humo del desayuno sobre el cielo
y pasa el tiempo
y esperamos y esperamos
y gruñimos
y no llega con las mazorcas
la muchacha vestida de rojo.

and now I write these lines and throw them into the waves
    in a bottle
because this is my story
because I am gazing at coconut trees and tamarinds
and mangos
the white sails drying in the sun
and the smoke of breakfast across the sky
and time passes
and we wait and wait
and we grunt
and she does not come with ears of corn
the girl in red.

La llamada

Cifar
calla tu canto.
Cifar
no recubras
de música tu oído:
Ese ilimitado
Azul
te llama.

The call

Cifar
quiet your song.
Cifar
do not cover
your ears with music:
That limitless
Blue
calls you.

Eufemia

"Et Merito, Quoniam Potui Fugisse Puellam . . ."

Tomé al azar la lancha de Pascasio
Y ahora reniego de mi suerte!
Miro las olas furiosas y los vientos
negros de Octubre ¡a qué horas
preferí este tiempo implacable
a la furia de Eufemia!
¿A qué puerto voy, a qué tumba
me lleva este chubasco perro?
Cuánto mejor aguantar
tus gritos, Eufemia; cuánto mejor
tu cólera, tu desgreñada
ira en la madrugada
que esta furia de las olas y estos gritos
bajo los rayos y los vientos!
Ya hubiera dominado tu enojo,
ya estuviéramos en los besos
ya dormiría dócil después de la tempestad
y no ahora, clamando a Dios
arrepentido, vomitando mi cobardía
en la borda, mientras el negro
cielo sólo me recuerda el furor de tus ojos . . .

Eufemia

"Et Merito, Quoniam Potui Fugisse Puellam . . ."

I happened to borrow Pascasio's boat
and now I curse my fate!
I look at the furious waves and the black
winds of October. At what moment
did I prefer this implacable weather
to Eufemia's fury?
To what port do I go, to what tomb
is this damned storm taking me?
How much better to bear
your screams, Eufemia; how much better
your anger, your disheveled
wrath at dawn
than the turbulent waves and these cries
under lightning and wind.
By now I would have managed your rage,
by now we would be kissing,
by now I would be sleeping calmly
after the storm;
instead I cry to God
repentant, vomiting my cowardice
over the rail while the black sky
only reminds me of your furious eyes . . .

La estrella vespertina

Vimos las llamas levantar la noche
y ensangrentar las aguas como un sol ahogado.
—¡Es la isla de Inés! —gritaron los marinos
y tiré la red y puse mano al remo
hundiéndolo en las aguas rojas.
Gritos se alzaban de ribera a ribera
y aves despertadas de sus nidos
giraban como cenizas.
¡Ya era tarde! Como una Y griega
escarlata escrita sobre mi sueño
la vi desnuda correr
y hundirse entre las olas.

       Hablo de Inés.
Siempre hablo de Inés
cuando la triste y vesperal estrella
baja a las ondas
y su desnudo ardor baña en las aguas.

The Evening Star

We saw the flames raise the night
and stain the waters with blood like a drowned sun.
—It's the island of Inés!—shouted the sailors
and I threw down the net and put my hands to the oars
plunging them into the red waters.
Cries rose up from shore to shore
and birds awakened from their nests,
circling like ashes.
It was too late! Like a scarlet Y
written on my dream
I saw her run
naked
and sink in the waves.

       I am speaking of Inés.
I always speak of Inés
when the sad evening star
goes down to the waves
and bathes its naked ardor in the waters.

El maestro de Tarca (III)

Maestro, dijo Cifar,
    seguí tu consejo
    y crucé el Lago
buscando la isla desconocida.
    Fui con viento benévolo
a la más lejana, virgen y perdida
        Pero
    que yo conocí esa isla
        juraría!
    que su sonoro acantilado
    devolvió mi canto un dia
        juraría!
    que era la misma mujer
la que allí me esperaba
        casi lo juraría!
Sonrió el maestro y dijo:
      Lo conocido
      es lo desconocido.

The Master of Tarca (III)

"Master," said Cifar,
     "I followed your advice
     and crossed the Lake
searching for the unknown island.
     I sailed with gentle wind
to the farthest one, virgin and lost
               But
          that I had known that island
          I would swear!
     That its sonorous cliff
     sent back my song one day
          I would swear!
     That she was the same woman
who waited for me there
          I would almost swear!"
The master smiled and said:
          "That which is known
          is the unknown."

Angelina en el acantilado

Pregúntame:
          —¿qué buscas
descalza
en las hirientes rocas
del acantilado?
          —¿Heriría
mis pies, subiría
con el viento y la lluvia
a divisar el lago
si el loco de Cifar . . .
          (y llora)
. . . vino a buscarme
y quiso
hacerme suya.
Me luchó sobre la arena
Le clavé
los dientes, le arañé
la cara y furioso
zarpó sobre el oleaje
a mitad de la borrasca.
—¡Ojalá no se pierda
en la tormenta!

¡Le estoy agradecida!

Angelina on the Cliffs

Ask me:
          —What do you look for
barefoot
on the jagged rocks
of the cliffs?
          —Would I gash
my feet, would I climb
in wind and rain
to scour the lake
if that crazy Cifar
     (and she weeps)
. . . he came looking for me
wanting
to have me.
He fought me to the sand;
I sank my teeth in him, scratching
his face and, furious,
he set sail over the waves
midway through a storm.
—I hope to God he won't be lost
in the storm!

I'm grateful to him.

Rapto

Sobre los cerros
en un cielo pálido
   brilla el lucero

Suelto el ancla y al ruido
chillan los pájaros
   Vuelan garzas
Los ganados balan
en el arenal lejano
De la choza
sale Fidelia peinándose
al fresco del alba

   Se vino anoche
   conmigo. Me dispararon
   tiros, me echaron
   lanchas veleras. Pero
   "La Sirena" corre.

Tengo una isla para ella.

Abduction

Over the hills
in the pale sky
a morning star
    shines.

I drop anchor; at the sound
birds screech
    herons fly
cattle bleat
on the distant dune.
From the cabin
comes Fidelia combing her hair
in the cool air of dawn.

    She came with me
    last night. They fired shots
    at me, set sailboats
    against me. But
    "The Siren" is fast.

I have an island for her.

Escrito en un árbol

De la verdad de la leyenda
doy ahora fé.

Marineros burlones me dijeron:
—Si le hablas
será trocada en árbol.

¡Vedme bajo su sombra!

Nunca el corazón
dio frutos tan numerosos!

Writing on a Tree

The truth of the legend
I swear to now.

Bantering sailors told me:
—If you speak to her
she will turn into a tree.

See me under its shadow!

Never has the heart
given so much fruit!

El maestro de Tarca (IV)

Dijo el maestro
de Tarca:

Coge la cigarra
del ala
Al menos
llevas en la mano
el canto.

The Master of Tarca (IV)

Spoke the Master
of Tarca:

Grasp the cicada
by the wing
At least
you carry in your hand
the song.

El niño

El niño
que yo fui
no ha muerto
     queda
     en el pecho
toma el corazón
como suyo
y navega dentro
     lo oigo cruzar
     mis noches
     o sus viejos
     mares de llanto
     remolcándome
     al sueño.

The Child

The child
I was
has not died
      he remains
      in my breast
taking my heart
as his own
and sails inside me
      I hear him cross
      my nights
      or his old
      seas of tears
      towing me along
      to dreams.

Calmura

Rogando al viento
Insultando al viento
hijueputeando al viento
o comprando al menesteroso
con la moneda rabiosamente
arrojada por la borda
        —¡Silba al haragán!
        —¡Grítale al viento!
        —¡Arréalo!
y silba agudo el marino
y revientan los adjetivos contra el duro
        SOL
que inmoviliza las aguas.
        Pero
        no responde la vela
        flácida
        como el ala de un ave muerta.

Arsenio, granuloso
cliente del burdel de Lalita
desesperado de calor
se tira al Lago. Y vemos
        la rápida
aleta del tiburón.

        Al grito de espanto
        como un eco
        aflora del fondo
        en silencio
        la mancha roja.

Dead Calm

        Begging the wind
        insulting the wind
        son-of-a-bitching the wind
or bribing the needy
with the money furiously
thrust over the gunwale
            —Whistle at the bum!
            —Shout at the wind!
            —Drive it!
and the sailor whistles sharp
and the adjectives burst against the hard
            SUN
that stills the waters.
            But
            the sail does not respond
            limp
            as the wing of a dead bird.

Arsenio, pimply
client of Lalita's whorehouse
crazy with the heat
throws himself into the Lake. And we see
            the swift
fin of the shark.

        At the scream of terror
        like an echo
        from the depths
        the red stain
        flowers
        in silence.

45

La isla vacía

Los árboles
que detenían la luna
oponen
todavía
su sombra
y nacen los mismos cantos
del viento
entre las ramas.
Junto al camino breve
de tu casa a las aguas
ya no está tu ropa
tendida, pero siguen
las flores. Todo es igual.
Sin embargo
lamento haber fondeado
en la arenosa
bahía
de tu isla.

The Empty Island

The trees
that were blocking
the moon
still
cast their shadows,
and the same songs are born
of the wind
among the branches.
Along the short path
from your house to the waters
your clothes are no longer
laid out, but
the flowers go on.
All's the same.
And yet,
I'm sorry I moored
in the sandy bay
of your island.

El maestro de Tarca (V)

Sentado en la piedra del Águila
el maestro de Tarca nos decía:

Es conveniente
es recto
que el marinero
olvide a las aguas
su aventura.
   Estela hecha
   tiempo vivido
   Estela deshecha
   tiempo borrado.

The Master of Tarca (V)

*Seated on the stone of the Eagle
the Master of Tarca would tell us:*

*It is fitting
and right
that the sailor
should leave his adventure
to the waters.*
> *Wake formed
> time lived
> wake dissolved
> time erased.*

Las bodas de Cifar

". . . y el mar virginicida batían con sus remos."
Licofrón.

—¡Deja de llorar! —gritaron las mujeres
y se oyeron sus risas
                        entre el reflejo
de las antorchas
                        y el golpe de los remos.
Llevaban a Ubaldina, con guitarras
con su velo de novia
y un ramo de azucenas.
Eladio, el carpintero de ribera
y Pascasio, el marinero manco
construyeron la barca.
Yo labré el mástil
                        y mi madre
cortó—sobre el arenal—la vela.
            Zarpamos
cuando rompían los albores
    pero Octubre
levantó los vientos.
Ráfagas, turbiones,
        olas
        rayos
el lago embravecido
y negro nos golpeaba a muerte
el barco y nos rompía
        las velas y las drizas.
Al caer de la tarde
    el huracán bramaba.

50

The Wedding of Cifar

". . . and they thrashed with oars the sea, killer of virgins."
                                        Lycophron.

—Stop weeping! cried the women
and we heard their laughter
                    by the reflection
of torches
                    and through the strokes of oars.
They were taking Ubaldina, with guitars
with her bridal veil
and a bunch of white lilies.
Eladio, the river carpenter
and Pascasio, the one-armed sailor
built the boat.
I worked the mast
                    and my mother
trimmed the sail on the sand.
          We set sail at dawn
    but October
raised the winds.
Squalls, torrents,
        waves
        lightning
the Lake
enraged
and black
struck to kill
tearing
        our sails and breaking our halyards.
At sunset
    the hurricane roared.

—¡Mierda! —gritó Eladio— ¡Nos hundimos!
Pero el viejo Pas, sereno
con su brazo único al timón
        dijo a los hombres:
—"Está el Lago cebado
la lancha es virgen
y la mujer doncella."
Abrieron entonces la escotilla y nos metieron
al oscuro vientre:
          olía
a brea el maderamen.
Tumbé a Ubaldina aterrada
y más que el amor
    las olas me ayudaron.
Después abrí la escota
saqué el brazo
y tiré el velo a las aguas.
    (Así engendré a Rugél
    tan duro en los peligros
    pero débil con las hembras.)

—Shit! cried Eladio. —We're sinking!
But the old man, Pas, serene
with his one arm at the helm
                    told the men:
—The Lake has swallowed
the bait,
the boat is a virgin,
the girl is a maiden.
Then they opened the hatchway and put us
into the dark belly:
                    the wooden hull
smelled of tar.
I pushed down the terrified Ubaldina
and—more than love—
        the waves helped me.
Then I opened the hatch,
put out my arm
and threw the veil into the waters.
        (So I begat Rugél
        a man so strong in danger
        but so weak with women.)

Consuelo para la madre del pescador

No des gusto
a las rugientes
olas llorando
su estrago:
devoraron a tu hijo
a traición—como el taimado
jaguar que nunca
se amansa a la caricia.
Ahora has conocido
al Alevoso.
                ¡Guárdate
de regocijarlo! Sus aguas
se alimentan
de lágrimas.

Consolation for the Mother of the Fisherman

Do not please
the roaring
waves by weeping
about their ravage:
they devoured your son
treacherously—like the sly
jaguar that never
is tamed with caresses.
Now you have known
the Traitor.
            Beware
of delighting him. His waters
feed
on tears.

Mi mujer es aquélla

La del pañuelo.
La que a veces mira
hacia mi lancha
y conversa
con las mujeres
como que no me ha visto.
Mi mujer es aquélla.
La que ahora se ríe
ahora
que el ancla cae
llenando de ecos la ensenada.

That's My Woman

The one with the kerchief.
The one who sometimes looks
toward my boat
and talks
with the women
as if she hasn't seen me.
That's my woman.
The one who laughs
now
that the anchor falls
filling the cove with echoes.

Despedida

Que las aguas te devuelvan
                  a la orilla
y llegues vomitando algas
y castañeteando los dientes
                  por el frío
            que te encuentre
            con la cara en la arena
tendido como un perro azotado por las olas
gritaba el corazón de la muchacha
mientras sus labios besaban al marinero.

Farewell

Let the waters send you back
      to the shore
and may you arrive vomiting seaweed,
your teeth chattering
      with the cold
  let me find you
  with your face in the sand
stretched out like a dog lashed by the waves
(cried the heart of the girl
while her lips kissed the sailor).

Viento en los arenales

La marazón
    arroja
  sardinas
a la costa.
Hiede la playa
     y vienen
gentes de adentro
con lámparas
    y hambre
   y suena
como un gemido
    el viento.

Wind on the Sand Dunes

The stormy sea
        hurls
    sardines
at the coast.
The beach stinks.
            And they come,
people from inland,
with lanterns
        and hunger,
    and the wind
sounds
            like a moan.

La carta

Me escribe Eufemia
que vuelva.
Yo le contesto: En tierra
repitiendo pisadas
abre caminos
el hombre.
Las aguas no tienen sendas.
    El Lago
      no guarda huellas.

The Letter

Eufemia writes,
inviting me back.
I answer: On land
repeating footsteps,
man opens pathways.
The waters have no paths.
The Lake
keeps no tracks.

Canto que hizo Cifar en la vela del angelito

Cuando se hundió
"La Esperanza"
todos perecieron.

Los que fuimos
al rescate
sólo vimos
—flotando—
el ataúd de un niño.

Song Composed by Cifar at the Wake of the Little Angel

When "The Hope"
sank
all perished.

> We who went
>> to the rescue
>> saw only
> the coffin of a child,
>> floating.

Papel a Cristóbal

Cristóbal:
        tu ahijado
está de nuevo entre rejas
sin dinero. ¿La culpa?
¡Ya lo sabes! ¡Eufemia!
Quise decir adiós
al pasado
pero volví los ojos
y vi a los pájaros
revoloteando sobre la estela.

Message to Cristóbal

Cristóbal:
       your godson
is behind bars again
without money. Who's to blame?
You know. Eufemia!
I wanted to say goodbye
to the past
but turned my eyes
and saw the birds
wheeling over the wake.

El rebelde

Todavía la aurora
no despierta el corazón
de los pájaros y ya Cifar
tira la red en el agua
oscura. Sabe que es la hora
de la sirena y no teme
el silencio.
             Cifar espera
la señal en las lejanas
serranías. Antes del alba
encenderán sus fogatas
los rebeldes.
             Les lleva peces
y armas.

The Rebel

Dawn has not yet
awakened the heart
of the birds, and already
Cifar casts his net into the dark
water. He knows it is the hour
of the siren, and does not fear
silence.
        Cifar waits
for a signal from the distant
mountains. Before dawn
the rebels will kindle
their bonfires.
          He takes them fish
and weapons.

Tomasito, el cuque

—¿En qué lancha las llevaron?
  ¡Contesta, Tomás, contesta!
—¿Desde cuál isla zarparon?
  ¡Jodido, Tomás, contesta!
—¿A quiénes las entregaron?
  ¡Hijo de puta, Tomás!
—¿Quiénes llevaron las armas?
  ¡Cabrón, contesta, Tomás!

Pero no habla Tomás.
¡Qué huevos de hombre. No habla!

  ¡Ya nunca hablará
  Tomás!

Tomasito, the Cook

—What boat did they carry them in?
    Answer, Tomás, answer!
—What island did they sail from?
    Damn it, Tomás, answer!
—Who'd they deliver them to?
    Son-of-a-bitch, Tomás!
—Who carried the weapons?
    You pimp, answer, Tomás!

But Tomás won't talk.
What balls! He doesn't talk.

    Now Tomás
    will never talk again!

Anades

Cuando al grito del hombre
se levantan
los cormoranes
y los piches
cagan su miedo
en las aguas
luego suben
vuelan
en
V
como una larga
flecha
arrojada al horizonte
recuperan
en la altura
el orden
la libertad
y el canto.

Ducks

When the cries of men
raise
the cormorants
and the ducks
shit their fear
in the waters
then they rise
and fly
in a
V
like a long
arrow
hurled at the horizon
recovering
at that altitude
order
freedom
and song.

Canción de la naciente luna

Una mujer desnuda
  ahogándose —grita—
  en las aguas

  Al recogerla
  en la lancha
  sus pezones tiemblan.

No se me borre nunca
esta hora, cuando
la naciente luna
iluminó a Mirna
en mi barca!

Song of the Rising Moon

A naked woman
  drowning, screams
  in the waters.

    When she's picked up
    in the barge
    her nipples tremble.

Let me never forget
this hour, when
the rising moon
illuminated Mirna
in my boat!

In memoriam

Juan de Dios
    Mora
(de los Mora
de Zapatera).
    Oviedo habla
del primer Mora
(criaba cerdos
con las sardinas
del Lago), Bovallius
habla de los Mora
y Squier. Siglos
de habitar la isla
        pero
    nunca dueños.
    Posando
    pescando
    fabricando
       redes
    y lanchas,
    saliendo siempre
de la tierra
    al agua
de la pobreza
a la aventura,
de la guitarra
    a la barca.

In Memoriam:

Juan de Dios
     Mora
(of the Moras
of Zapatera).
     Oviedo speaks
of the first Mora
(he used to raise hogs
on sardines
from the Lake). Bovallius
speaks of the Moras
and Squier. Centuries
of living on the island
        but
     never owners.
       Lodging
       fishing
       making
         nets
       and boats,
always going
from land
     to water
from poverty
to adventure,
from guitar
    to boat.

Hoy vuelve
el navegante.
     Sus huesos
en una caja
     de madera.
¡Su único
naufragio
en tierra!

Today the sailor
returns.
His bones
in a wooden box.
His only
shipwreck
on land!

La isla de los "Gavilanes"

Los "Gavilanes"
abandonaron esta isla.
(Juan era timonel del "barco."
Alfonso el más diestro
pescado de sábalos. Felipe
el dueño de "La Sirena"
la más rápida velera
de estas aguas.
Hoy Juan maneja un taxi
en Managua y cobra
un peso por carrera
Alfonso es dipsómano perdido
Felipe es el dueño
del burdel "La Sirena.")

The Island of the Gavilanes

        The Gavilanes
        abandoned this island.
    (Juan was helmsman of the "boat,"
    Alfonso the most skillful
    fisherman of shad, Felipe
    owner of "The Siren,"
    the fastest sailing ship
        in these waters.
    Today Juan steers a taxi
    in Managua and charges
    one peso a ride.
    Alfonso is a hopeless drunk.
        Felipe owns
      a whorehouse, "The Siren.")

Nostalgia de Cifar

"A veces la lancha
huele a muelle"
dijo Cifar, añorando
a Fidelia, deseando
volver al hogar y ver
al hijo que ya remaba en las islas.
Regresaban los cormoranes
volvían las garzas
chillando en busca de sus nidos.

Cifar's Nostalgia

"At times the boat
smells of piers"
said Cifar, yearning
for Fidelia, wishing
to go back home and see
his son who was already rowing in the islands.
The cormorants were returning,
and the herons
squawking
in search of their nests.

Mirna

Llamando perras
a las violentas olas
insultando al negro
viento del poniente
rompió dos veces la vela
y atravesó el temible
    playón de Enero
porque Mirna, la prostituta
le esperaba en el puerto.

Mirna

Calling
the violent waves
bitches,
insulting
the black west wind,
he tore the sail twice
and crossed the terrible
    shallows of Enero
because Mirna, the prostitute,
waited for him in port.

La desgracia

En Alta Gracia
me enredé en un pleito
de cantina. *El Arpero*
está preso.
Me comprometieron
las mujeres
y herí a un hombre.
       —¡Traigan a ese jodido!
Me llevaron.
El herido
era el hijo del Alcalde
       ¡Es en la celda, amigos,
       donde nacen los tangos!
Ahora mis queridos
compañeros
se avergüenzan.
Eufemia
no quiere ni saber cómo me llamo
Fidelia está muy lejos
y mi madre muerta.
Sólo Mirna
se escapa del burdel
y me trae comida.

Misfortune

In Alta Gracia
I got into a fight
at the saloon. *The Harpist
is in jail.*
Involved
with the women,
I wounded a man.
          —*Get that bastard!*
They took me away.
The wounded man
was the Mayor's son.
          Jail, my friends,
          is where tangos are born.
Now my dear
mates
are ashamed of me.
Eufemia
doesn't even want to know my name.
Fidelia is very far
and my mother is dead.
Only Mirna
sneaks out of the whorehouse
and brings me food.

El maestro de Tarca (VII)

El maestro de Tarca
    me decía:

    la Alegradora
con su cuerpo da placer,
no con su recuerdo.

    Con la mano hace señas
    con los ojos llama,
no con su recuerdo.

La Alegradora
    es el puerto
    la tierra
    que sólo es del pobre
    en la noche.

The Master of Tarca (VII)

The Master of Tarca
        would tell me:

        The Alegradora
pleases with her body,
not with her memory.

        With her hands she beckons
        with her eyes she calls,
not with her memory.

The Alegradora
        is the port
        the land
        that belongs to the poor
        only at night.

La procesión

Doce doncellas
de blanco
en el bote enramado
—cantan y reman—
Le sigue
el bote de cedro
de Venancio Arana
con arcos de flores
y doseles
de palmas
    doce muchachos
    remeros
      y el Sacramento
y luego
los botes isleños
y las gentes
cantando
    "Allá van las tres Marías
    orilladas a la mar . . ."
Es el jueves
de Corpus
y Ubaldina
mi hija
va de blanco
cantando.

    ¡Me río de Cifar
    que está llorando!

The Procession

Twelve girls
in white
on a boat covered
with flowers
sing and row.
Next comes
Venancio Arana's
cedar boat
with arcs of flowers
and canopies
of palms
    twelve young
    oarsmen
       and the Blessed Sacrament
and then
the island boats
and the people
singing
    "There go the three Marias
    bordering the sea . . ."
It is the Thursday
of Corpus Christi
and Ubaldina
my daughter
goes in white
singing.

    I laugh at Cifar
    who cries!

Piolín

A Pitín

Una isla
picoteada
por las gallinas
—un pedazo
de estrella—fue
el país
de Piolín
        el niño
        de los gallos.

A la vela
llega Magdaleno
                vela
de cuerpo ausente
—el remo del niño
y cuatro candelas—
—"Piolín:
                salvaste
a la niña Rina
salvaste a Teo
        mi hijo!"

Tocan violines.
        Lloran
        alto
    las abuelas
y los pescadores
    con lámparas
buscan el cuerpecito

Piolín

To Pitín

An island
pecked
by hens
—a piece
of star—was
the country
of Piolín
    the child
    of the roosters.

Magdaleno arrives
at the vigil
over an absent body
—the child's oar
and four candles—
—"Piolín:
        you saved
the child Rina
you saved Teo
    my son!"

Violins play.
      Grandmothers
      weep loudly
and the fishermen
  with lanterns
search for the little body.

Entonces
canta el gallo
de Piolín:
—¿Dónde estará?—

(La noche llena de gallos)

—¿Dón-de-es-taraaá?
De isla
en isla
los gallos preguntan
por el niño
y con preguntas
van haciendo
el alba.

Then
Piolín's rooster
crows
"Where can he be?"

(The night is filled with roosters.)

"Where ca-a-a-n he be-e-e-e?"
From island
to island
the roosters ask
about the child
and with questions
they were making
the dawn.

Lo que escribió Cifar sobre su hija Ubaldina

Me diste ¡oh Dios! una hija con el cielo
de mi patria en sus ojos;
no el azul de la indolente calmura
sino el oscuro
fragor
de la tormenta.

Me diste, ¡oh Dios! una hija con el espíritu
de la barca
en que crucé las aguas
enfurecidas del tiempo.
No permitas, Señor! que el viento
la arroje como a mí
a lo insaciable.

Dale una bahía mansa
donde se refleje su barca
como empollando
otra barca, una ensenada
donde el sol
seque sus redes.

Written by Cifar about His Daughter, Ubaldina

To Milagros

You gave me
oh God!
a daughter with the sky
of my country in her eyes,
not the blue of the lazy dead calm
but the dark din
of the storm.

You gave me
oh God!
a daughter with the spirit
of the boat
on which I crossed
the furious waters of time.

Lord! do not let the wind
hurl her
as it hurled me
to the ravenous one.

Give her a gentle bay
where her boat will be reflected
as if hatching another,
a peaceful inlet
where the sun
will dry her nets.

El cementerio de los pájaros

Arribé al islote
enfermo
fatigado el remo
buscando
el descanso de un árbol.
      No vi tierra
      sino huesos.
De orilla a orilla
huesos
y esqueletos de aves,
plumas calcinadas,
hedor
de muerte,
moribundos
pájaros marinos,
graznidos
de agonía,
trinos tristes
y alguna
trémula
osamenta
aún erguida
con el pico
abierto al viento.
Con débil brazo
moví los remos
y dí la espalda
al cementerio
del canto.

The Cemetery of the Birds

I arrived at the barren island
sick
the oar weary
seeking rest
under a tree.
         I didn't see earth
         only bones.
From shore to shore
bones
and skeletons of birds,
calcined feathers,
stench
of death,
dying
sea birds,
caws
of agony,
sad trills
and a few
quivering skulls
still erect
with beaks
open to the wind.
With weak arms
I moved the oars
and turned my back
on the cemetery
of song.

Las islas

a Ernesto Cardenal

Llamo a mis amigos.
"Hagamos algo," les digo.
Pero todos se van,
    todos dispersos
    buscan lo suyo.
En Cárdenas
    en Orosí
        en San Miguel
no ha despuntado el alba
y ya prenden sus motores
o izan velas.
        "¿Qué busca
    de puerto en puerto
    mi pueblo?"
    ¿Hacia dónde
    enfila su proa
    el corazón de los pobres?

He navegado con ellos.

Vienen
soportando el tiempo
cargados de hijos
    y de animales
con guitarras y lámparas
cruzando
la densa marejada
hacia las islas.

The Islands

To Ernesto Cardenal

I call my friends together.
"Let's do something," I tell them.
But they all go,
    scattered,
    seeking their own way.
In Cárdenas
    in Orosí
        in San Miguel
dawn has not broken
and already they're starting their motors
or hoisting their sails.
      "What do my people seek
    from port to port?"
    Where
    does the heart of the poor
    point its prow?

I have sailed with them.

They come
enduring the weather
laden with children
    and animals
with guitars and lanterns
crossing
the dense surf
toward the islands.

(De este país
no quedan sino islas.)

Oigo
sus cantos.

Pascasio
nos habla de la muerte
la compañera de las aguas.
Eladio se ilusiona
con la pesca. Anselmo
hace cuentas con los dedos
y el Maestro de Tarca,
haciendo historia, nos dice:
—En Solentiname,
archipiélago de las codornices,
pereció Tamagastad
contra los escollos de la Venadita.
Allí lloró la tribu a su héroe.
Allí todavía lloran los que pasan
esperando una antigua promesa.
Allí dice la leyenda
que ha de volver a su pueblo
con una palabra nueva.

Se oyen lejanos
los gallos.
El viento
sopla en la brasa del lucero.
Parece
que ya amanece.

        (Nothing remains
        of this country but islands.)

                I hear
            their songs.

Pascasio
speaks to us of death,
companion of the waters.
Eladio is excited
by the fishing. Anselmo
counts on his fingers
and the Master of Tarca,
remembering history, tells us:
—In Solentiname,
archipelago of the quails,
Tamagastad did perish
against the reefs of Venadita.
There the tribe wept for its hero.
There those who pass by still weep
awaiting an ancient promise.
There, legend says,
he is to return to his people
with a new word.

            The cocks
        are heard in the distance.
            The wind
blows on the hot coal of the morning star.
Already it seems to be dawn.

Del maestro de Tarca (X)

Con el oído atento
al fragor de las olas
y los vientos,
el Maestro de Tarca
nos decía:

> En el rencor del Lago
> me parece oir
> la voz de un pueblo.

From the Master of Tarca (X)

With ear attentive
to the roar of the waves
and the winds,
the Master of Tarca
would tell us:

> In the rancor of the Lake
> I believe I hear
> the voice of a people.

Mujer reclinada en la playa

No ajena a la melancolía
Casandra me profetiza la gloria
y el dolor, mientras la luna
emana su orfandad.

Todo parece griego. El viejo Lago
y sus hexámetros. Las inéditas
islas y tu hermosa cabeza
—de mármol—
mutilada por la noche.

Woman Reclining on the Beach

*No stranger to melancholy
Cassandra prophesies for me glory
and pain, while the moon
reveals her orphanhood.*

*Everything seems Greek. The old Lake
and its hexameters. The unpublished
islands and your beautiful head
—of marble—
mutilated by the night.*

Pescador

Un remo flotante
      sobre las aguas
fue tu solo epitafio.

Fisherman

An oar floating
    on the waters
was your only epitaph.

Notes

In *Songs of Cifar,* Pablo Antonio Cuadra uses a diction that at once approximates common speech and is heightened to capture a tone reminiscent of Homer and other epic poets. His use of the two levels of diction—at times shifting between them and at other times fusing them in a remarkable way—is suited to his depiction of present life in a framework of Greek myth. Throughout the book, the names are real, and many of the details are biographical.

Dedication v

"Cifar Guevara," "Juan de Dios Mora." Examples of the curious but real names of people of The Lake region.

"Sweet Sea": *Mar Dulce.* It is translated here to mean fresh or sweet water, and also to convey the implication of "dear sea." It refers to Lake Nicaragua, which is so large that it is often called a sea.

"The Cockroach": *El Cachero,* a nickname without any literal meaning. It is rendered as "The Cockroach" to capture the sound of *El Cachero.*

The Birth of Cifar 5

"The shallows": *Playón,* which means, in this case, a large area of shallow water.

"The sailor": *El navegante,* translated as "the sailor" because it is used here and elsewhere as one who spends most of his time in the water, rather than one who masters navigation.

"Sharks and shad." Although it is sweet water, Lake Nicaragua actually has these creatures.

Horses in the Lake 7
"Soaring back / to the heroic days. . . ." Thus translated to keep the suggestiveness of the verb *remontar*.

"White stallions": *potros blancos,* used to mean a horse that is about to strike, as in the painting by Delacroix.

The Sickness 13
"One / sail / afar / is enough." Here as elsewhere, the attempt was to stay close to the literal meaning because of the two levels of diction throughout the book.

The Master of Tarca (I) 19
"Stone of the Eagle": *La Piedra del Águila* is a real stone located on an island named Tarca. Here Cuadra uses the myth of the oracle, joining it to a Nicaraguan setting.

The Girls 21
"Greet them": *Diles adiós,* which has this meaning here.

Manuscript in a Bottle 25
"And we grunt." The reference is to Circe and the pigs.

Abduction   37

"Abduction": *Rapto*. Translated as abduction, although Fidelia went on happily. The word "abduction" suggests Helen of Troy, whose image is suggested in this poem and in others of the cycle.

Dead Calm   45

"Dead Calm": *Calmura*. The word is nautical Nicaraguan language of the Lake.

"Son-of-a-bitching": *Hijueputeando,* a common swear word.

"The needy": *Menesteroso,* referring to the Lake.

"Drive it!": *Arréalo* is a word used in cattle droving, employed here as a metaphor. The poet is using Lake folklore. The people believe that a dying wind will pick up again if they throw a coin into the water. The sailors whistle at the wind, as well.

The Wedding of Cifar   51

Lycophron was a third-century Alexandrian Greek poet and grammarian, author of *Cassandra* (or *Alexandria*), from which the epigraph was taken.

"Killer of virgins": *virginicida*. Cuadra discovered that the people of the Lake have a myth that is analogous to that of Lycophron's passage: The Lake, like the sea of Lycophron's poetry, hates virgins. Hence, "they thrashed with oars the sea, killer of virgins."

"—The Lake has swallowed / the bait. . . ." The virgin-killer waters are compelled to kill by so much virginity.

113

"River carpenter": *Carpintero de ribera,* meaning a carpenter who works near the shore, building small boats.

Song Composed by Cifar at the Wake of the Little Angel 65

"Little Angel": *Angelito,* an affectionate term for a small child who dies before he can speak.

Misfortune 87

"Tangos": Songs of Argentinian origin, usually about fights between men over women.

The Master of Tarca (VII) 89

"The Alegradora": *La Alegradora,* which means, literally, a woman who makes others happy.

The Procession 91

"Allá van las tres Marías . . ." is the opening of a song traditionally sung by the Lake people on the Thursday of Corpus Christi.

Piolín   93
"Vigil / over an absent body": *Vela de cuerpo ausente.*
Cuadra sharpens the tragedy of Piolín's death by contrasting
the image of a "vigil / over an absent body" with the usual
act of *misa de cuerpo presente,* a funeral mass in which the
body is in view.

A. Z.

Glossary

Alta Gracia. Principal town of the Island of Ometepe.

Cárdenas, Orosí, San Miguel. Small ports on the edge of Lake Nicaragua.

Bovallius. Carl Bovallius (1849–1907), a Swedish zoologist who traveled throughout Central America in the 1880s. He was interested especially in the Island of Zapatera in Lake Nicaragua, and made precise drawings of the Pre-Columbian "idols" and pottery on that island. Those drawings appear in his book, *Nicaraguan Antiquities*, which was published in 1886 by the Swedish Society of Anthropology and Geography in Stockholm.

Harp. Music is mentioned often in this work, especially in relation to Cifar, "the harpist." His harp, of a type no longer in existence, is a primitive version of the stringed instrument we know.

The Lake, Great Lake, Sweet Sea. See the Introduction.

Oviedo. Gonzalo Fernendez de Oviedo, a Spanish chronicler who arrived in Nicaragua in 1527.

Tarca. One of many small islands in Lake Nicaragua. The "Stone of the Eagle" is a real stone here. In the "Master of Tarca" poems, Cuadra uses the myth of the oracle in the context of a Nicaraguan setting.

Solentiname. An archipelago of islands at the southern end of Lake Nicaragua, near the Costa Rican border. In 1966, Ernesto Cardenal, poet and priest, founded a small religious community called Our Lady of Solentiname on the largest of these islands, Mancarrón.

Squier. E. G. Squier (1821–88), representative of the United States to the country during the nineteenth century, is

117

the author of *Nicaragua: Its People, Scenery, Monuments and the Proposed Inter-Oceanic Canal.*

Tamagastad. The Nicaraguan name for Quetzalcoatl, "the feathered serpent." Tamagastad is the culture hero and god of the Toltecas, Nahuas, and Nicaraguas. According to legend, he will return to live with the people.

Venadita. One of the islands of the archipelago of Solentiname.

Zapatera. The Island of Zapatera, or "The Shoemaker Island," is one of two large bodies of land in Lake Nicaragua. Its name derives from the Pre-Columbian custom of burying the dead in shoe-shaped clay vessels. The island was an important religious center.

Books by Pablo Antonio Cuadra:
A Selected Bibliography

Poems

Poemas nicaragüenses. Santiago: Editorial Nascimiento, 1934. Second edition, revised, 1935. (Poems 1930–33.)

La Tierra prometida. Edited by Ernesto Cardenal. Managua: El Hilo Azul, 1952.

Libro de Horas: Antología de la poesía católica del siglo XX. Edited by Emilio del Río. Madrid: A. Vasallo, 1964.

El Jaguar y la luna. Managua: Editorial Artes Gráficas, 1959. (Author's private edition of seventeen poems with his own illustrations.) Second and first complete edition, Buenos Aires: Ediciones Carlos Lohlé, 1971.

Zoo. San Salvador: Dirección General de Publicaciones del Ministerio de Educación, 1962.

Poesía. Madrid: Ediciones Cultura Hispánica, 1964. (Author's selection from his earlier work, 1929–62.)

Tierra que habla: Antología de cantos nicaragüenses. San José: Editorial Universitaria Centroamericana, 1974. (Author's selection from his poems, 1929–71.)

Esos rostros que asoman en la multitud. San José: Ediciones El Pez y la Serpiente, 1976. (Poems 1963–67.)

Prose

Promisión de Mexico y otros ensayos. Mexico: Editorial Jus, 1945.

119

Entre la cruz y la espada: mapa de ensayos para el redescubrimiento de América. Madrid: S. Aguirre, 1946.
Torres de Dios, ensayos sobre poetas. Managua: Ediciones de la Academia Nicaragüense de la Lengua, 1958.
El Nicaragüense. Managua: Editorial Unión, 1967.
Otro rapto de Europa (Notas de un viaje). Managua: Ediciones El Pez y la Serpiente, 1976.

Drama
Por los caminos van los campesinos. Managua: Ediciones El Pez y la Serpiente, 1972.

(Note: In addition to these published books, many of the author's contributions to periodicals have been reprinted in separate bound volumes that have appeared from 1943 to 1977.)

A. Z.